Savannah
Figures It Out

by
Jeryl Christmas

This Book Belongs To

_____

Savannah studies **similes**
that REALLY don't make sense
and VERY silly **idioms**
that have her "on the fence."

Should she try to use them?
She'll decide at the end
if she figures out their usefulness
and if she'll recommend.

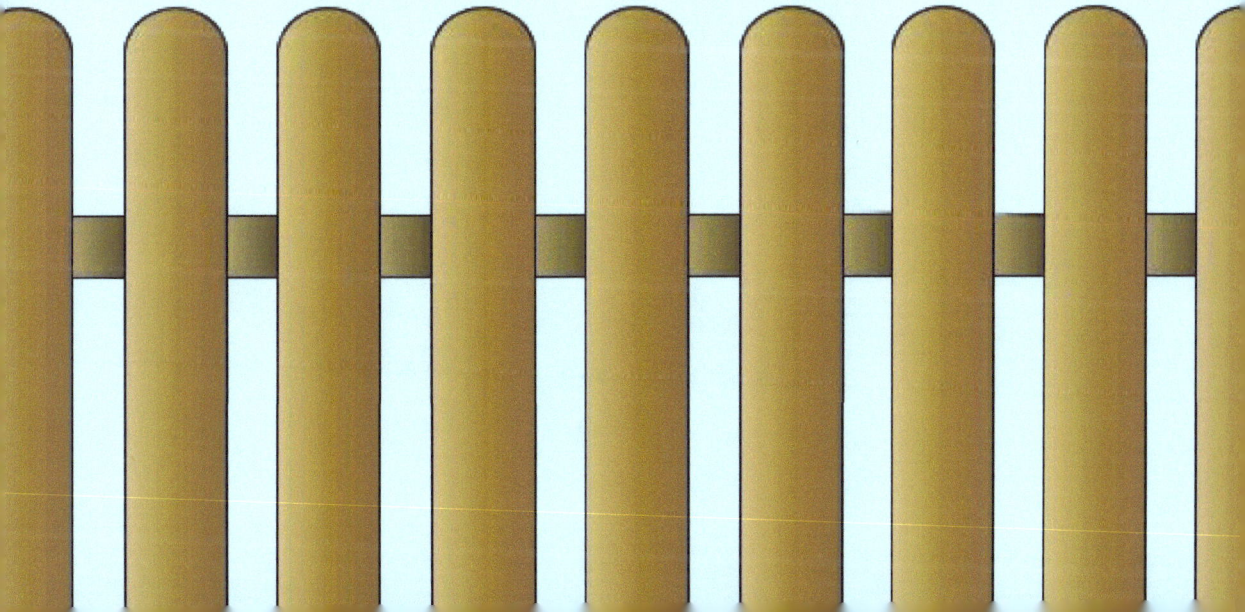

Is a fiddle really fit?
Is a bone ALWAYS dry?
Is every peacock proud,
and can pigs REALLY fly?

Is spilled milk worth the crying?
Should a towel be thrown in?
If a chip is on your shoulder,
should you have a thicker skin?

Is a goose really silly?
Are whistles always clean?
Is Christmas really slow?
Why does envy make you GREEN?

Why's a needle in a haystack?
Can't an OLD dog learn new tricks?
Does a donkey really have to work
THIS hard to "get his kicks"?

Are cats and dogs the preference
when it's raining very hard?
Can it ever rain **SPAGHETTI**
in your very own backyard?

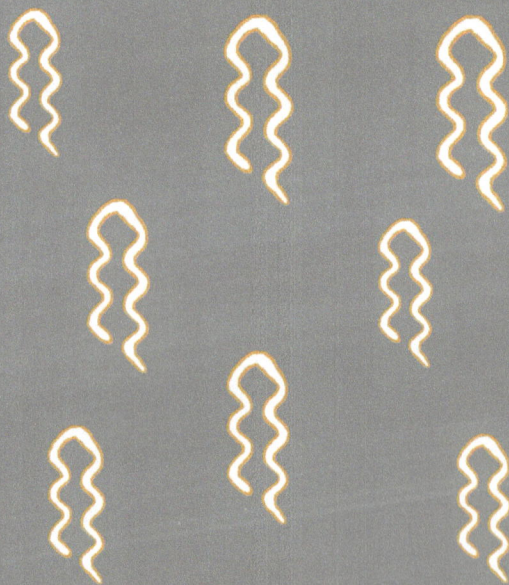

If lots of pots are boiling,
are you "cooking up a storm,"
or if your hands are cold,
does that mean your heart is warm?

Can a dog bark up the RIGHT tree?
Can a cat stay IN the bag?
Can a LATE bird get a worm?
Can you ZIG when you should zag?

Are two birds in a bush
really LESS than one in hand?
If that makes any sense at all,
I just don't understand.

Can you wake up with the chickens?
Can you rise with the sun?
Do monkeys in a barrel
really have the best of fun?

Are clams really happy?
Are arrows always straight?
Do GOOD things really come
to those who simply sit and wait?

Are bats really blind?
Can't they see things eye to eye?
Would you REALLY want an ointment
that is sold with a fly?

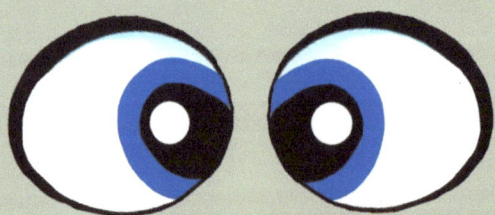

Are bees ALWAYS busy?
Can logs really sleep?
Whenever would a wolf
want to dress up like a sheep?

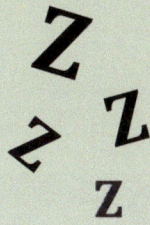

Is pie really easy?
Are pins ever neat?
Does a rose by any OTHER name
really smell as sweet?

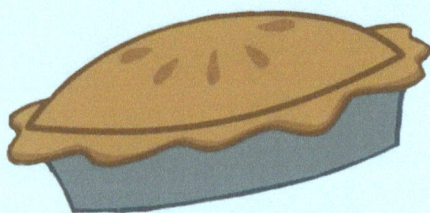

Are mice always quiet?
Are owls REALLY wise?
Can something that seems bad
be a blessing in disguise?

If your eggs are in ONE basket
and your bottom dollar's spent,
aren't you taking quite a risk
when you don't have one RED cent?

If something "costs an arm and leg,"
isn't that a crime,
especially when a DOZEN things
are sold for just a dime?

10¢ each

Dime a Dozen

Dime a Dozen

Dime a Dozen

Why is something very easy
often called "a piece of cake,"
and WHYEVER would you tell
someone "go jump in a lake"?

What is a ballpark figure?
When is something "for the birds"?
Sometimes common phrases
are just SIMPLY, SILLY words!

SO, what did Savannah figure out?

When it comes to figurative language,
always think "OUTSIDE the box."
NEVER take it literally.
Be as "clever as a fox."

Your writing will be colorful
and interesting to read.
Your **idioms** and **similes**
will "do the trick," INDEED!

The End

Savannah's Similes

1. **Fit as a fiddle**-being in good health
2. **Dry as a bone**-completely dry
3. **Proud as a peacock**-overly proud
4. **Silly as a goose**-very foolish
5. **Clean as a whistle**-spotless
6. **Slow as Christmas**-taking a long time
7. **Happy as a clam**-very content
8. **Straight as an arrow**-completely honest
9. **Blind as a bat**-having bad eyesight
10. **Busy as a bee**-very active
11. **Sleep like a log**-sleep very soundly
12. **Easy as pie**-very simple
13. **Neat as a pin**-very clean
14. **Quiet as a mouse**-silent, without noise
15. **Wise as an owl**-using good judgment
16. **Clever as a fox**-very clever or intelligent

Savannah's Idioms

1. **On the fence**-undecided
2. **When pigs fly**-something unlikely to happen
3. **Don't cry over spilled milk**-don't worry about things in the past
4. **Throw in the towel**-give up
5. **Chip on one's shoulder**-angry attitude believing one has been treated unfairly in the past
6. **Thick skin**-an ability to keep from getting upset by things people do or say
7. **Green with envy**-very jealous
8. **A needle in a haystack**-something hard to find
9. **You can't teach an old dog new tricks**-you can't make someone change an old way of doing something
10. **Get your kicks**-do something you enjoy
11. **Raining cats and dogs**-raining very hard

12. **Cooking up a storm**-doing a lot of cooking at once and with a lot of energy
13. **Cold hands, warm heart**-one who doesn't outwardly show feelings but is really very kind and loving
14. **Barking up the wrong tree**-having a wrong idea
15. **Let the cat out of the bag**-tell a secret
16. **Early bird gets the worm**-the first to arrive is more successful
17. **Zig when one should zag**-misstep or mess up
18. **A bird in the hand is worth two in the bush**-it's better to hold onto something than risk losing it
19. **Wake up with the chickens**-wake up at a very early hour
20. **Rise with the sun**-get out of bed at sunrise
21. **More fun than a barrel of monkeys**-funny and enjoyable
22. **Good things come to those who wait**-be patient when trying to achieve your goals
23. **See eye to eye**-agree with each other
24. **A fly in the ointment**-something spoiling a situation
25. **Wolf in sheep's clothing**-one who pretends to be good but is really trying to do harm
26. **A rose by any other name smells the same**-what something is called doesn't change its characteristics
27. **A blessing in disguise**-a good outcome from a bad situation
28. **Don't put all your eggs in one basket**-don't put all your efforts in one thing
29. **Bottom dollar**-your last dollar
30. **One red cent**-tiny amount of money
31. **Costs an arm and leg**-very expensive
32. **A dime a dozen**-very inexpensive
33. **A piece of cake**-very easy
34. **Go jump in a lake**-an angry way to tell someone to go away
35. **A ballpark figure**-near the exact amount
36. **For the birds**-worthless
37. **Think outside the box**-explore ideas in a creative way
38. **Do the trick**-achieve what you want
39. **Come alive**-become energized